Beyond the Glass

Bon Appétit!

Dayna Seely

Beyond the Glass

BOURBON RECIPES FROM HORSE COUNTRY

by The Kentucky Spirited Chef | Dayna Seelig

ISBN 978-0-692-18685-5

Cover design and book layout by
Jeffrey Liles, Mound Marketing & Communications LLC

Photography by
Kat Wagers, Kat Wagers Studios
Dylan Lambert, Dylan Lambert Photography

Additional food photography by
Dayna Seelig

Published in association with
IngramSpark

Note to reader: Cup measurements in this book are for U.S. cups. Teaspoons are 5 ml and tablespoons are 15 ml. Temperatures are in Fahrenheit degrees. Conversion charts can be found in the index. All cooking times are an approximate guide only. Unless otherwise stated, milk is assumed to be whole, eggs are large and pepper is freshly ground black pepper.

Disclaimer: This book assumes the reader does not suffer from any food allergies or related medical conditions. Anyone with a food allergy should avoid recipes that contain ingredients which could cause an adverse reaction in the reader or anyone who will eat the prepared food.

This publication is intended only for responsible adults of legal drinking age in the U.S. (21 years old or older). It is intended solely for entertainment purposes. The author and publisher do not advocate or encourage the abuse of alcoholic beverages. Please drink responsibly and with moderation. Please do NOT drink and drive. We do not, under any circumstances, accept responsibility for any damages that result to yourself or anyone else due to the consumption of alcoholic beverages.

Although the author and publisher have made every effort to ensure that the information in this book was correct at press time, the author and publisher do not assume and hereby disclaim any liability to any party for any loss, damage, or disruption caused by errors or omissions, whether such errors or omissions result from negligence, accident, or any other cause.

Acknowledgements

A big thanks to the official taste testers Gayle Baskey, Patsy Watts, Becky Priest, Amber Fraley, Terry Fraley, Jeffrey Liles, Carmen Liles, Margaret King, Katherine King, Pam Murphy and my mom Carol Spencer for their generous compliments and constructive feedback. Your love for food and all things Bourbon made the taste test successful and the most fun I have had cooking for people in a very long time.

A loving thank-you to my sons, Rian and Justin, who asked for a family recipe that caused me to find the treasure trove of delicious recipes hidden in a date book which started this whole adventure. Thank you to my family for adventuresome tasting of all my new creations.

Thank you to photographer Kat Wagers for taking the most delicious and creative photos in some of the most unusual settings!

A very special thank you to Lena Hedberg for allowing us to spend time at her gorgeous Hedberg Hall, Inc. farm, taking photos and getting to know the beautiful thoroughbreds and foals.

It is with special appreciation that I thank Jeffrey Liles for editing, layout and design expertise, and guidance throughout the whole publishing process. Without his generosity, expertise and support this book would not exist.

Thank you to Carmen Liles for providing thoughtful suggestions, as well as accepting "Dayna's door-to-door dessert delivery service".

And thank you to all of the individuals who pick up this book and are inspired to make one of the recipes. I hope you enjoy preparing and sharing them with friends and family as much as I have enjoyed creating them.

Dedication

I dedicate this book to my very loving husband, Mike, for supporting my adventures in cooking and always declaring each item I cook his favorite. You are my best friend in the world and champion taste-tester. You are the best sous-chef anyone could ever imagine. I love and appreciate you more than you will ever know.

—Dayna

Hedberg Hall, Inc., Mount Sterling, Kentucky

Bourbon and horses are hallmarks of Kentucky and the Bluegrass region. The Kentucky Bourbon distilleries provide the chef with many Bourbon brands recognized worldwide which enhance and extend flavors in a variety of recipes.

Within this book, many selections came from a family recipe book dating from the early 1900s to the 1940s, including some multi-generational recipes dating before 1900.

All recipes are carefully chosen and tested Bourbon dishes that have been perfected through the years. They are guaranteed to become new favorites of your family and your guests – all proven to have them asking for more!

Contents

Introduction

Kentucky has a rich southern heritage that blends culinary arts from many diverse cultural backgrounds.

I was raised in Lexington and on a horse farm in nearby Fleming County, Kentucky. The traditions of Kentucky Bourbon and wonderful country food were a part of my life from childhood. My grandmother and mother cooked and baked with Bourbon before it became the current world-wide phenomenon.

Many of the older recipes use seasonal foods with the freshest flavors as well as those foods that could be canned or cured.

My sons, Justin and Rian, remembered an old chili sauce recipe that their great-grandmother Spencer made to be used on potatoes, beans and in chili. I started searching for the recipe, and found my grandmother's handwritten recipe book that included many of her mother's, mother-in-law's and grandmother's recipes.

Finding that recipe book, written on a 1939 yearbook, started a creative journey.

I noticed many of the old recipes did not include vanilla in the ingredient list for baked goods. There was a notation on one of the pages that indicated a teaspoon or tablespoon of Bourbon would enhance the flavor of the dish.

I began experimenting with the historic recipes, including Bourbon in them and sometimes substituting Bourbon for other flavors listed in the recipes. The end results are what I consider to be a collection of company-worthy dishes and baked goods.

I hope you will enjoy!

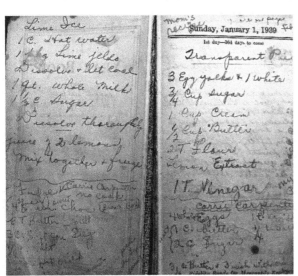

Grandmother Spencer's recipe book.

Dayna with her mother in the kitchen.

Bourbon Bacon BBQ Meatballs

Meatballs

2 lbs of 80/20 ground beef

1 tsp salt

2 Tbsp black pepper

2 Tbsp powdered garlic

3 Tbsp liquid smoke

2 eggs

**1 cup panko bread crumbs
(or ¼ cup chopped chia or flax seeds)**

1 small package of real bacon pieces

Bourbon BBQ Sauce

16 oz bottle of your favorite smoky BBQ sauce

¼ cup Bourbon

¼ cup dark brown sugar

1 Tbsp minced garlic

1 tsp salt

2 Tbsp pepper

1 Tbsp liquid smoke - hickory

1 Tbsp smoked paprika

**8 slices of bacon cooked and crumbled
(or use 1 small package of real bacon pieces)**

I held a formal taste test for many of the recipes in this book and the individuals were instructed not to talk until all critiques had been submitted for each food. But the non-verbal sounds, raised eyebrows and smiles on their faces gave away how much they enjoyed the flavors of the meatball in their mouth.

Mix together the meatball ingredients.

Form walnut sized meatballs (or slightly smaller for one bite appetizers).

Bake on a foil-lined cookie sheet in the oven at 350 degrees until done. Do not overcook or the meatballs will be tough.

Remove and drain on paper towels.

Mix together the Bourbon BBQ Sauce ingredients.

Put the meatballs and sauce together in a large pan.

Cook on top of the stove on low to medium for about 10 minutes. Make sure you stir often or the sauce will stick.

The sauce and meatballs could be placed in a large crockpot instead of stirring on top of the stove.

When I take these meatballs to a party as an appetizer or serve them to guests at home I usually make a double batch because they disappear quickly. It always amazes me after the meatballs are gone my guests will still scoop up the sauce and eat it, too! They freeze well - *but don't count on leftovers!*

Fudge Pie with Bourbon Raspberry Jam

1 deep dish pie crust

1 ¼ cups of heavy whipping cream

5 Tbsp butter

½ tsp salt

2 large eggs

6 Tbsp Bourbon

1 pint raspberries or 1 cup cherry pie filling

⅔ cup of raspberry jam or cherry preserves

9 oz 60% cacao chocolate chips

TIP: You may need to heat the jam depending on its consistency. You can also put it in the food processor if the chunks of fruit are very large.

Preheat oven to 325 degrees.

Use your favorite pie crust recipe or use a prepared rolled crust from the store. Place the pie crust in a deep-dish pie pan. Do not pre-cook.

Mix 1/3 cup of jam with 2 Tbsp Bourbon.

Spread 1/3 cup of raspberry bourbon jam (or cherry preserves if you prefer) in a thin layer on the bottom of the pie crust.

In a large sauce pan heat heavy whipping cream, butter and salt until just bubbling. Remove from stove.

Add 9 oz of 60% cacao chocolate chips to the whipping cream mixture. Let it sit for a few minutes until the chocolate melts.

Whisk the chocolate until it is thick and fully incorporated into the cream.

Add 2 Tbsp bourbon, whisk well.

Add the two eggs one at a time. Use the whisk to blend until smooth.

Place the chocolate mixture into the pie crust over the jam

Cook until it is almost firm in the middle.

Refrigerate until cool.

Before serving this pie, spread with 1/3 of either raspberry or cherry jam with 2 Tbsp Bourbon and top with either fresh raspberries or 1 cup of cherry pie filling.

Refrigerate any leftovers.

Chocolate Bourbon Dream Cake

1¾ cups of water

⅓ cup Bourbon

2 packets of your favorite coffee shop's instant Italian dark roast coffee or 1 Tbsp espresso powder

6 oz of dark chocolate unsweetened, at least 72% cacao, chopped into small pieces

2 sticks salted butter, also chopped

2 cups sugar

2 cups all-purpose flour

1 tsp baking soda

½ tsp salt

2 large eggs, beaten

2 tsp vanilla extract

Bourbon Pecan Glaze

1 cup light corn syrup

¼ cup sugar

½ stick butter (¼ cup)

¾ cup Bourbon soaked chopped pecans (¾ cup nuts and ½ cup Bourbon)

For glaze: Combine first three ingredients and stir over medium heat until sugar is dissolved, for about 1 minute after a rolling boil begins. Remove from heat and add ¾ cup of Bourbon soaked chopped pecans. Drizzle ½ over the cake now and reserve ½ to spoon over individual pieces when served.

Preheat oven to 300 degrees. This recipe can be made as a Bundt, or mini-Bundt cakes with equal success. Coat the pans with baking spray that includes flour.

In a medium pan, combine water, Bourbon and instant coffee (or espresso) powder on medium heat for about 2 minutes or until a rolling boil. Reduce to low heat and add the chocolate and butter that has been chopped into small pieces. Once the chocolate and butter have dissolved and the liquid is smooth remove from the heat.

Add sugar and stir until the sugar has dissolved. Stir in the vanilla. Transfer to a large bowl.

Combine flour, baking soda and salt in a small bowl. Then add half of the flour mixture to the chocolate and beat well with a mixer. Keep adding the flour mixture until smooth. Add the eggs. Beat for another minute at high speed.

Place batter in prepared pan. Bake for about 75 minutes until knife inserted into cake comes out clean. If using the small Bundt pans watch for the tops to set. Start checking at about 20 minutes. Make sure the cakes fully cool before removing them from the pan. Makes about 12 servings.

I am not a cake person and I rarely eat cake. I never order it out. I do love chewy cookies and pies, and this cake is so moist I love, love it plain. Of course I *really* love it with Bourbon sauce, which I also use as the base for the chocolate raspberry cream cheese cake, Bourbon ball cake and Yule log recipes you'll find in this book. I confess – my husband and I eat it with our coffee in the morning. I have not found a recipe that is so moist and decadent – and is even better after it has been frozen for a couple of days. I never use any other recipe when I make chocolate cake!

—Dayna

It was always a treat when my grandmother made a cake. Each one was always moist and the aroma coming from the kitchen spread throughout the house. She had to keep telling us not to open the oven or we would spoil the cake. That didn't always stop us – and it never spoiled her cakes. These two dream cake recipes use her basic white and chocolate cake recipes, and I have added some extra flavors to enhance the deliciousness of her two recipes. I know the recipe says to wait to cut the Chocolate Dream Cake until it cools – but it smells so good that we end up scooping it out with a spoon while it is hot and adding a bit of Bourbon ice cream. It's so good and so decadent! (Just slice the rest when it cools.)

TIP: Unlike the chocolate with raspberry version which you can scoop out as described above, be sure the blueberry recipe is cooled completely before it is cut. The filling will be a problem to cut if it is not cool. Serve drizzled with Creamy Bourbon Sauce found on page 73.

Dream Cake
with Blueberry and Cream Cheese filling

Cake

½ **stick of butter, melted**

1 cup sugar

1 egg

2 cups all purpose flour

2 tsp baking powder

1 cup half & half

1 Tbsp Bourbon Cream

Filling

8 oz cream cheese, room temperature

1 cup sugar

1 egg

2 tsp Bourbon

Prepare two 9 inch round cake pans with baking spray or butter and flour. Cream butter and sugar. Add egg and Bourbon Cream. Mix well. Add dry ingredients and mix well. Add half & half. Mix with hand or stand mixer for 3 minutes.

For filling: Cream the ingredients until fluffy.

Pour cake batter into pan. Place spoonfuls of filling evenly across cake. Use knife to make swirls. Sprinkle cake evenly with two cups of fresh blueberries. Using your palm, press blueberries into cake.

Bake at 350 degrees for 40-50 minutes until a knife comes out clean. Top with Creamy Bourbon Sauce.

Chocolate Dream Cake
with Raspberry and Cream Cheese filling

Cake

1 ¾ cups of water

⅓ cup Bourbon

2 packets of your favorite coffee shop's instant Italian dark roast coffee or 1 Tbsp of espresso powder

6 oz dark chocolate unsweetened, at least 72% cacao, chopped into small pieces

2 sticks salted butter, chopped into pieces

2 cups of sugar

2 cups all-purpose flour

1 teaspoon of baking soda

½ tsp of salt

2 large eggs, beaten

2 tsp vanilla extract

Filling

8 oz cream cheese, room temperature

1 cup sugar

1 egg

2 tsp Bourbon

I small jar or can of Raspberry pie filling (you can substitute jam but not jelly)

TIP: Before starting the cake, soak 12 Tbsp of chopped pecans in 8 Tbsp of Bourbon.

Prepare 13x9 cake pan with baking spray.

In medium pan, combine water, Bourbon and instant coffee powder on medium heat for 2 minutes or until a rolling boil. Reduce to low heat and add chocolate and butter. Once chocolate and butter have dissolved and liquid is smooth remove from heat.

Add sugar and stir until dissolved. Stir in vanilla.

Combine flour, baking soda and salt in a small bowl. Then add half of the flour mixture to the chocolate and beat well. Keep adding the flour mixture until smooth. Add eggs. Beat for 1 minute at high speed.

Cream the filling ingredients until fluffy.

Pour cake batter into prepared pan. Place spoonfuls of filling evenly across the cake. Drop 1 tsp of raspberry pie filling on top of each cream cheese dollop. Use knife to make swirls. You can add coconut, nuts and/or dark chocolate chips sprinkled on top of cake if you desire before baking.

Bake at 300 degrees for about 40-50 minutes. If you want a creamier filling do not over bake.

A friend mentioned she could eat the inside of the Bourbon Balls like icing. I thought it would be a great idea to marry two of my favorite recipes together — Chocolate Bourbon Cake and the creamy filling of the Bourbon Balls. It tastes so much better than I even hoped! I love chocolate, so I covered it with my favorite icing — dark chocolate ganache.

Bourbon Ball Cake

Cake

1¾ cups of water

⅓ cup Bourbon

2 packets of your favorite coffee shop's instant Italian dark roast coffee or 1 Tbsp of espresso powder

6 oz dark chocolate unsweetened, at least 72% cacao, chopped into small pieces

2 sticks salted butter, also chopped

2 cups sugar

2 cups all-purpose flour

1 tsp baking soda

½ tsp salt

2 large eggs, beaten

2 tsp vanilla extract

Bourbon Ball Icing

½ cup of Bourbon-soaked chopped pecan mixture (see tip)

¼ cup softened, not melted, butter

8 oz confectioners sugar

Chocolate Ganache

½ cup whipping cream

1 cup dark chocolate chips

1 Tbsp light corn syrup

1 tsp Bourbon

TIP: Prepare Bourbon-soaked chopped pecan mixture for icing at least 2 days before making cake. Add 1½ cups Bourbon to cover 2 cups finely chopped pecans. Seal in a jar or container with lid.

Use my Chocolate Bourbon Dream Cake recipe on page 13, but bake cake in two loaf pans. If you bake the cake in one loaf pan, it will overflow and the cake will not be as moist. Remove the cooled cakes from the pans. Wrap in wax paper and then aluminum foil. Freeze the cake for one day.

Take the cake out of the freezer and let it thaw slightly. Slice the cakes into two equal horizontal layers. You will use the two bottom layers and one top layer to make the cake. Reserve and freeze the other top layer to serve with ice cream and raspberries for another quick dessert.

Mix the center icing ingredients, divide in half for each layer. You should have enough for both layers. Spread the icing in between the three layers of the cake.

Ice the cake with Chocolate Ganache.

Add decorative pecans to the top of the cake. Keep the cake in the refrigerator and serve in slices.

Baked Brie with Apricots and Walnuts

1 wheel or wedge of brie soft-ripened cheese

4 Tbsp apricot preserves

4 Tbsp Bourbon
(or 2 Tbsp for a lighter Bourbon taste)

6-8 chopped walnuts

2 green apples, sliced thin

12 oz crostini or your favorite crackers

This recipe is my go-to when I have company drop in. I always have a round of brie in the refrigerator and nuts in the cupboard as well as preserves. I have also used cherry jam with slivered almonds and raspberry jam with pecans.

I must admit I have destroyed baked brie heated in the oven while trying to transfer it to a serving plate. I use the microwave instead of the oven to soften the brie right on the dish I plan to serve it on. There's no messy transfer from a hot oven to the serving plate – and it's much quicker, too.

Cut the rind off the top of the brie.

Place the brie on a microwave safe dish that you can use for serving.

Soften the brie for about 1 minute on high in the microwave.

Remove brie from the microwave.

For topping, mix these two ingredients together thoroughly:

4 Tbsp of apricot preserves

2 Tbsp of Bourbon (light Bourbon taste)
- or -
4 Tbsp Bourbon (strong Bourbon taste)

Place mixture on top of the brie and finish with rough chopped walnuts.

Serve with crostini or crackers and thin green apple slices.

TIP: Your guests will still enjoy this treat if you serve it with room temperature Brie.

Bourbon Turtles

1 lb roasted pecans

2 pkgs dark chocolate melting wafers for candy making and dipping

Bourbon Caramels

2 cups sugar

2 sticks butter

2 cups heavy cream

1½ cups light corn syrup

3 Tbsp Bourbon

Bourbon caramels are candy I used to make every Christmas. Each family member got a tin of caramels, which means I made at least 6-8 batches. That was a lot of cutting and wrapping.

One night I ran out of wax paper that I used to wrap each individual caramel. I was trying to figure out how I could finish making the candy without the wrappers – and came up with the idea for Bourbon Turtles.

They were such a hit I no longer have to wrap caramels anymore – because they all want the turtles! The roasted pecans add a dimension you do not get with store-bought candies and it really makes a difference in taste.

Prepare a large platter with butter.

For the Bourbon Caramels, place the sugar, butter, heavy cream and corn syrup in a very large pan.

TIP: Use a large pressure cooker without the lid. A Dutch oven is not large enough.

Cook on high heat, stirring often until mixture changes from creamy to light caramel color. Turn heat down to medium. Stir often and cook to soft ball stage.

Take off stove and stir in 3 Tbsp of Bourbon. Stir until caramel stops bubbling. Pour onto prepared platter and let it cool until it can be cut without running.

Place parchment paper on countertop or on a cookie sheet. Place 3-4 whole pecans together for each turtle with ends touching. Place one cut caramel in the middle and slightly press onto the caramel until it secures all the pecans. Repeat for each turtle.

Melt dark dipping chocolate in the microwave according to the directions. Do not burn the chocolate. Use a teaspoon to drizzle the chocolate over the turtles.

Store in a cool place, but not the refrigerator or the nuts may become soggy.

Bourbon Bacon BBQ Meatloaf

Meatloaf

2 lbs of 80/20 ground beef

1 tsp salt

2 Tbsp black pepper

2 Tbsp powdered garlic

3 Tbsp liquid smoke

2 eggs

**1 cup panko bread crumbs
(or ¼ cup chopped chia or flax seeds)**

½ of the Bourbon BBQ Sauce (recipe below)

Bourbon BBQ Sauce

16 oz bottle of your favorite smoky BBQ sauce

¼ cup Bourbon

¼ cup dark brown sugar

1 Tbsp of minced garlic

1 tsp salt

2 Tbsp pepper

1 Tbsp liquid smoke - hickory

1 Tbsp smoked paprika

**8 slices of bacon cooked and crumbled
(or use 1 package real bacon pieces if in a hurry)**

Preheat oven to 350 degrees.

Mix together the Bourbon BBQ sauce ingredients.

Combine the meatloaf ingredients, being careful to use only half of the Bourbon BBQ Sauce.

Form a loaf and place on a foil lined cookie sheet.

TIP: Instead of putting bread on the bottom of the loaf as some chefs do, I put two half slices of bread on either side of the loaf to soak up the excess fat).

Cook in 350 degree oven until the meatloaf is firm – about 40 minutes.

Add the remainder of the Bourbon BBQ Sauce and allow the meatloaf to cool for 10 minutes for easier slicing.

Kentucky Bourbon Chocolate Nut Pie

⅓ cup melted butter

½ cup white sugar

¼ cup dark brown sugar

1 Tbsp Bourbon

¾ cup light corn syrup

Pinch of salt

3 whole eggs

¾ cup dark chocolate chips

5 oz of rough chopped walnuts or pecans

Your favorite deep dish crust recipe
(or frozen pie shell)

Preheat oven to 350 degrees. Prepare a deep pie dish pie crust but do not pre-cook the crust.

TIP: I always place aluminum foil on a cookie sheet under this pie.

Melt butter.

Add sugar, corn syrup and Bourbon and use a hand mixer to blend well.

Add the salt and eggs and again blend well.

Spread the chocolate chips and nuts (your choice) evenly on the bottom of the crust.

Pour the filling evenly on top of the chocolate chips and nuts.

Bake at 350 degrees for about 40-55 minutes depending on your oven. You should remove the pie when the center of the pie is set and doesn't move when lightly shaken.

TIP: I bake on the middle rack. Depending on your oven you may have to move it to the bottom rack if the crust begins to get too brown.

Wait until cool to cut, otherwise the slices will fall apart. (Read the wording under the photograph for the technique I really use!)

This pie is a special day pie – and not the special day of the first Saturday in May. On July 5, Mike makes this pie for my birthday, and honestly any other time I can get him to make it! I prefer the walnuts to pecans, but the pecans are more traditional. In the recipe, I caution to wait until it cools to cut it, but I am always impatient and end up eating it like cobbler with ice cream...the first slice anyway!

Bourbon Hawaiian Chicken

6-8 boneless, skinless chicken thighs, cut into large pieces

2 cups large diced green peppers

3 cups of pineapple chunks well drained and excess moisture removed

Bourbon Marinade

¼ cup olive oil

¼ cup soy sauce (use low sodium if you desire)

¼ cup pineapple juice

½ cup Bourbon

¼ cup light corn syrup

½ cup dark brown sugar

2 heaping Tbsp of minced garlic

1 tsp salt

Preheat oven to 375 degrees.

Combine the marinade mixture.

Add remaining ingredients except the pineapple into the marinade mixture.

Bake covered for 20 minutes.

Remove from oven and add pineapple to the dish, stirring well.

TIP: The pineapple can be grilled before adding to the dish for extra flavor.

Bake uncovered for an additional 5 minutes. Baste often to ensure the sauce is evenly distributed.

Serve with rice.

Garnish according to your taste: sesame seeds, green onions.

I always felt something was missing when I was eating Bourbon chicken over rice. I had Hawaiian chicken with pineapple and thought it was missing something, too. So... I combined the two, added green peppers and found the recipe my family loves.

Cupcake Surprise

Use my Chocolate Bourbon Dream Cake recipe (found on page 14)

Cupcake Filling

8 oz cream cheese

½ cup sugar

1 egg, beaten

3 Tbsp drained chopped cherries (prepared overnight - see tip below)

½ cup dark chocolate chips

Bourbon Cream Cheese Icing

8 oz cream cheese

⅓ cup softened - not melted - butter

3-4 cups confectioners sugar

The rest of the maraschino cherries and the Bourbon used for soaking

TIP: Soak 12 maraschino cherries in 1/8 cup Bourbon overnight before making these special cupcakes.

The original cupcake recipe has been a favorite in my family since my grandmother made them for me. This is more of a grown up version of "Black Bottom Cupcakes" – with a cherry bourbon surprise in the center and in the icing!

—Dayna

Using my Chocolate Bourbon Dream Cake recipe, fill cupcake papers no more than 2/3 full.

For filling: Using a mixer, beat the first 4 cupcake filling ingredients until the mixture turns white and fluffy. Add chocolate chips.

Put 1 heaping tsp of mixture in the center of each cupcake.

Bake in 350 degree oven until the white center looks set but not hard. This will be like cheesecake.

Do not take cupcakes out of the papers until completely cool.

For icing: Using a mixer, beat all icing ingredients until fluffy. Icing will be light pink. Spread generously on cool cupcakes.

Cherry Bourbon Truffles

8 oz of dark chocolate chips or dipping chocolate

¼ cup heavy whipping cream

12 maraschino cherries soaked overnight in 2 Tbsp Bourbon

Unsweetened dark cocoa powder

I keep some of these, a batch of my Bourbon Turtles and a few Bourbon Balls in the refrigerator during the holidays to quickly make a dessert plate for drop-in company. They are also included in a small tin for a hostess gift when we are guests of others.

TIP: The night before making these truffles, chop 12 maraschino cherries into small pieces and cover them with 2 Tbsp Bourbon in a small cup.

Heat the heavy whipping cream in a bowl in the microwave for one minute.

Pour the dark chocolate chips into the bowl when it is removed from the microwave. Stir until all of the chocolate chips have melted.

Add the maraschino cherries and stir well.

Cover the bowl and place it in the refrigerator for 2-3 hours.

Once it is chilled you can scoop it out with a melon ball scoop. Shape each truffle into a ball and roll it in the dark cocoa powder.

Place it on wax or parchment paper on a cookie sheet.

Once all are rolled into balls and dusted, place the cookie sheet in the refrigerator to set the candy.

You can also roll the truffles in coconut or chocolate sprinkles for a different version.

Store in the refrigerator until ready to serve. Makes about 15 truffles.

Bourbon BBQ Chicken

6 boneless, skinless chicken thighs
(you can use 8 tenderloins if you prefer white meat)

Bourbon BBQ Marinade

8 oz bottle of your favorite smoky BBQ sauce

¼ cup Bourbon

¼ cup dark brown sugar

1 Tbsp of minced garlic

1 tsp salt

1 Tbsp pepper

1 Tbsp liquid smoke

1 Tbsp smoked paprika

8 slices of bacon cooked and crumbled
(or use one package of real bacon pieces)

Preheat the oven to 375 degrees.

TIP: You may want to line your casserole dish with aluminum foil as this dish gets very sticky.

Bake the chicken uncovered for 15 minutes while you prepare the marinade.

After 15 minutes add the marinade to the chicken, making sure all pieces are coated.

Cook for another 10-15 minutes depending on the size of the chicken pieces. Stir one more time halfway through to coat evenly.

Add 2 Tbsp Bourbon after it is finished if you want a stronger bourbon flavor in the sauce in the pan. Recoat chicken with the sauce before serving.

Serve with rice, corn, fried potatoes, baked potato, slaw or salad.

We love using the extra sauce as a "gravy" for mashed potatoes. I always make a large batch and freeze half for another meal. Makes the chicken tender, flavorful and Bourbon-licious!

Apple Walnut Bread Pudding with Bourbon Sauce

Apple Walnut Bread Pudding

Loaf of cinnamon bread, cut into 1 inch cubes

½ cup (1 stick) butter

5 large eggs, beaten

1½ cups whole milk

1½ cups whipping cream

1½ cups sugar (try brown sugar)

2 Tbsp cinnamon

5 Tbsp Bourbon

2 cups chopped Jonathan apples (about 3 large apples) - use soft apples so they melt into the bread

1½ cups chopped walnuts

TIP: I use cinnamon bakery bread. If you don't have cinnamon bread you can use Hawaiian bread or French loaf – but you will need to add 4 Tbsp of cinnamon when you toss the bread with butter.

Bourbon Cream Sauce

4 oz cream cheese

2 Tbsp melted butter

1 cup confectioners sugar

¼ cup Bourbon

For sauce: Using a mixer, cream all four ingredients together and drizzle over the bread pudding. If it is a bit stiff, try putting in the microwave for 10 seconds at a time.

Preheat oven to 350 degrees. Grease a 13x9 inch baking dish.

Cut the bread into 1 inch cubes. In a large bowl toss with melted butter. (Remember to add the extra cinnamon if you are using the alternate bread.)

Layer bread, then apples, and walnuts in at least two layers.

Combine milk, cream, sugar and cinnamon in medium pan. Heat over low heat until sugar is dissolved.

Use a whisk and slowly add eggs and Bourbon to the hot milk mixture and mix until smooth.

Take it off the stove and pour the hot mixture over the bread and let it stand for about 15 minutes.

Top with ½ cup of chopped walnuts.

Bake for 30 minutes covered loosely with foil. Remove foil and bake for another 30 minutes until the bread is set and the top is golden brown.

It is my fantasy to open a bed and breakfast, except I love to travel so much myself that it probably isn't in the cards. But our friends wake up to a wonderful smell in the morning when they stay with us. I always love a dish you can prepare the night before, so I can have time to enjoy my company. We eat bread pudding and breakfast casseroles on Christmas morning, so everyone can have "lazy time" and move slowly that day with their favorite coffee or tea.

Chocolate Croissant Bread Pudding

12 regular size croissants

Custard Mixture

½ cup (1 stick) melted butter

1 cup sugar

4 ½ Tbsp ground cinnamon

¼ cup Bourbon

5 large eggs, beaten

2 ½ cups whipping cream

12 regular size croissants

1 cup of chopped pecans (½ cup per layer)

1 cup dark chocolate chips (½ cup per layer)

Bourbon Cream Sauce

4 oz cream cheese

2 Tbsp melted butter

1 cup confectioners sugar

¼ cup Bourbon

For the Bourbon cream sauce, use a mixer to cream all 4 ingredients together. Then drizzle over the bread pudding. If it is a bit stiff, try putting it in the microwave oven for 10 seconds at a time. Enjoy!

Preheat oven to 350 degrees.

Prepare a 13x9 baking dish with butter.

Cut the croissants into 1-inch cubes and put ½ of croissant cubes as the first layer in the pan. Sprinkle ½ of the pecans and chocolate chips over the top of the croissant pieces.

Repeat above steps for the second layer.

For custard mixture, combine sugar and butter in a medium saucepan.

Add eggs, Bourbon and cinnamon. Use a hand or stand mixer to blend well.

Add the whipping cream to the mix and blend well.

Pour the mixture over the croissants, pecans and chocolate and let it stand for about 15 minutes. Make sure all the croissant pieces are covered by the custard mixture. Press any pieces that are not covered down into the mixture.

Bake for 35 minutes covered loosely with foil. Remove foil and bake for another 15 minutes until the middle of the bread pudding is set, but soft and the top is golden brown.

Mount Sterling's Farm to Table Dinner

When my husband and I travel I always look for chocolate croissants. They are one of my favorite decadent treats. And where did I find my absolute favorite? Right here in Mount Sterling, Kentucky! Spoonful of Sugar has the lightest croissant oozing with dark chocolate – better than any I have had in Europe. So why wouldn't it work in a bread pudding? It does! I could eat the whole pan in a couple of days. Mike and I keep slicing slivers throughout the day and forget about eating regular meals until it disappears. It is even better with the Bourbon cream sauce drizzled over it. *What a great way to start – or end – the day!*

Bacon BBQ Bourbon Baked Beans

1 can of your favorite brand of baked beans, smokehouse flavor

½ lb browned and drained ground beef

½ cup diced onions

2 Tbsp yellow mustard

1 16 oz bottle of your favorite smoky BBQ sauce

¼ cup Bourbon

¼ cup dark brown sugar

2 tsp salt

2 Tbsp pepper

1 Tbsp liquid smoke - hickory

8 slices of bacon cooked and crumbled (Use one package of real bacon pieces if you are in a hurry).

Be sure to reserve half of the bacon to place on top of the casserole.

Combine all of the ingredients, stir well and place in a baking dish.

Top with the reserve bacon.

Bake at 350 degrees until the center is hot and bubbling.

Our family doesn't have a picnic, BBQ, church lunch or summer potluck without these beans. I always double the recipe and the corners of the pan are scraped clean. We have also been known to use it on top of hot dogs as coney sauce.

This recipe was a favorite at our taste testing. The guests all needed larger sized tasting dishes!

This coffee cake without the icing hits the spot for our guests who are "not breakfast people". The chocolate/toffee center is just the sweet touch many people crave in the morning. Served with coffee, our guests don't realize this can also be used as a dessert if you add the caramel nut topping.

Toffee Cake with Bourbon Nut Icing

Pound Cake

1½ cups butter, softened

1 cup dark brown sugar, packed

1 cup light brown sugar, packed

1 cup granulated sugar

5 large eggs

3 cups all-purpose flour

1 tsp baking powder

½ tsp salt

1 cup half & half

8 oz bag chocolate toffee chips

1 cup roasted pecans, chopped fine

Bourbon Nut Icing

14 oz can sweetened condensed milk

1 cup brown sugar

2 Tbsp butter

6 Tbsp Bourbon-soaked chopped pecans

For icing: Combine milk and brown sugar in medium sauce pan and bring to a boil over medium-high heat stirring constantly. Reduce heat and simmer for 8 minutes, stirring frequently. Remove from heat and add butter and Bourbon-soaked pecans. Let cool for 2-3 minutes. Drizzle on the cake while the topping is still hot.

TIP: *Before starting cake, soak 6 Tbsp chopped pecans in 6 Tbsp of Bourbon and set aside. Prepare the cake ahead of time, then prepare the topping. Cake needs to cool completely before removing from pan.*

Preheat oven to 325 degrees. Spray a tube or Bundt pan with baking spray, or grease the pan and dust with flour.

For cake: Cream butter and 3 sugars until fluffy. Add in the eggs. Add flour, baking powder and salt. Mix well. Add milk and beat until just combined.

Put 1/3 of the batter in the pan. Make a trench and place ½ of the toffee chips and pecans distributed evenly. Make sure the trench is made for each layer so the toffee chips do not stick to the side of the pan when done.

Repeat with another 1/3 of the batter and the remaining chips and pecans. Top with the last 1/3 of the batter.

Bake for about 75 minutes or until a toothpick or knife comes out clean. You may need to cover the cake with foil to reduce excess browning.

Allow cake to cool completely before removing from pan or it will break apart.

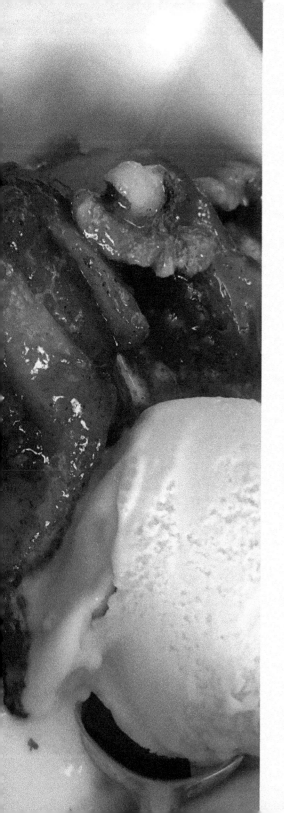

Baked Apples in Bourbon Butter Sauce

3 large firm apples

4 Tbsp dark brown sugar

3 Tbsp butter, melted

1 Tbsp cinnamon

2 Tbsp Bourbon

Core and peel apples. Cut apples in quarters.

Combine brown sugar, melted butter, Bourbon and cinnamon in bowl. Place apples in bowl and stir until the sauce has covered all apple pieces.

Place apples in a deep baking pan that has been coated with butter cooking spray or butter.

Cover with foil and bake at 375 degrees for 20 minutes.

Remove foil and bake at 375 degrees for about 15 minutes or until the apples are tender. Serve while hot.

TIP: This recipe can be served as either a side dish or dessert. To serve as dessert:

Combine 4 Tbsp brown sugar, 2 Tbsp of flour, 2 Tbsp butter, 2 Tbsp Bourbon, 1 tsp cinnamon, ½ tsp salt, ¼ cup finely chopped walnuts. Spread this mixture evenly over the apples. Bake at 400 degrees for 10 minutes on the top rack.

Fresh Fruit Dip

8 oz cream cheese

1 cup confectioners sugar

Choose one of the following to flavor the dip:

½ cup fresh cherries or raspberries chopped fine

¼ cup Bourbon

Best served with apples and/or strawberries and pineapple.

- or -

⅛ cup brown sugar

¼ cup Bourbon cream

1 Tbsp maple syrup

Best served with apples. Great for fall with tart new apples!

Place cream cheese, sugar and your choice of flavoring in a mixing bowl.

Blend using a mixer or food processor to make sure everything is creamed.

Cherry Crisp with Bourbon

3 cups of fresh or canned cherries

¼ cup of Bourbon

Topping

1 stick butter, softened

1 cup white sugar

½ tsp salt

¾ cup of flour

1 Tbsp cinnamon

Preheat oven to 350 degrees.

Prepare an 8x8 pan with spray or butter to keep cherries from sticking.

If using fresh cherries, cut them in half. If using canned cherries, drain the juice.

Soak the cherries in the Bourbon for 30 minutes. Your company will thank you for taking a few extra minutes for this step!

Place the cherries in the bottom of the pan.

Soften the butter.

Mix all of the other ingredients together before adding them to the butter. Cut into the butter until it is crumbly.

Bake until the topping is brown and the cherries on the bottom are bubbling.

Serving suggestions: Ice cream, sliced almonds, and of course my chocolate Bourbon sauce. My husband Mike is always handy with an ice cream scoop!

Company is coming and I need dessert! This can be in the oven in less than 15 minutes and out of the oven in less than 40. Cherry is my favorite. But I also use blackberries or peaches when they are in season because the topping is perfect for any ripe fruit that pairs well with Bourbon.

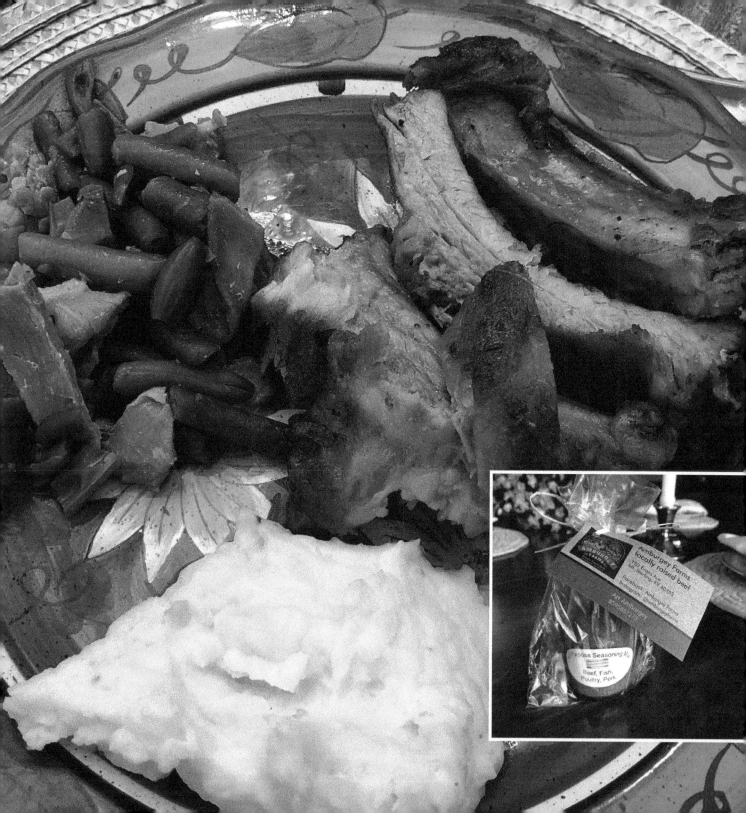

Amburgey Farms
locally raised beef
130 Evans Ave
Mt. Sterling, KY 40353
Facebook: Amburgey Farms
Instagram: @amburgeyfarms

Purpose Seasoning Mix

Beef, Fish,
Poultry, Pork

Matt's Masterpiece Ribs

My brother loves to cook as much as I do and his specialty is creating tender meat dishes.

—Dayna

2 long racks of ribs (pork or beef- your choice)

4 oz Dijon mustard

2 Tbsp liquid smoke

2 Tbsp Bourbon

8 oz dark brown sugar

**4 oz of your favorite dry rib rub
(I use Amburgey's All Purpose Rub)**

15 oz bottle of your favorite smoky BBQ sauce

8 oz apple juice

TIP: These ribs can also be finished on the grill for a bit of char. 3 minutes each side.

Peel membrane off back side of ribs. Cut any visible excessive fat off ribs. Mix Dijon mustard, liquid smoke and Bourbon together and brush on ribs, coating evenly. This will allow the rub to stick.

Mix brown sugar and dry rub together and evenly coat both sides of ribs making sure to push down gently so it adheres. Wrap in plastic wrap and refrigerate overnight.

Get pan with lifted cooking rack for baking. This will allow the heat to surround the ribs and cook evenly. Place 8 ounces of apple juice under the cooking rack. Remove the plastic and place ribs, meat side up, on cooking rack.

Turn on broiler and broil ribs for about 5 minutes until slightly browned and they start to bubble. Then cook at 300 degrees for one hour and 15 minutes, uncovered.

After cooking this initial time, place tin foil tightly over pan and cook additional one hour and 15 minutes.

Then, open foil and brush BBQ sauce on both sides of ribs, recover and bake an additional 30 minutes.

Once done, allow ribs to sit covered for about 10 minutes. Uncover and enjoy!

Smoked Creamy Bourbon Sweet Potatoes

2 cups heavy cream

3 Tbsp dark brown sugar

4 Tbsp Bourbon

1 Tbsp liquid smoke

3 large sweet potatoes, peeled and sliced ⅛ inch thick

Salt and pepper to taste

Preheat oven to 375 degrees.

Spray a 9x9 inch baking dish.

Whisk together cream, brown sugar and Bourbon until smooth.

In prepared dish, arrange the potatoes in ten even layers. Between each layer, use 3 Tbsp of the cream mixture and season with salt and pepper.

Repeat with remaining potatoes, cream, and salt and pepper for all 10 layers.

Cover and bake for 30 minutes.

Remove cover and continue baking for 45 minutes to 1 hour. Cream should be absorbed, the potatoes should be cooked through and the top should be beautifully browned.

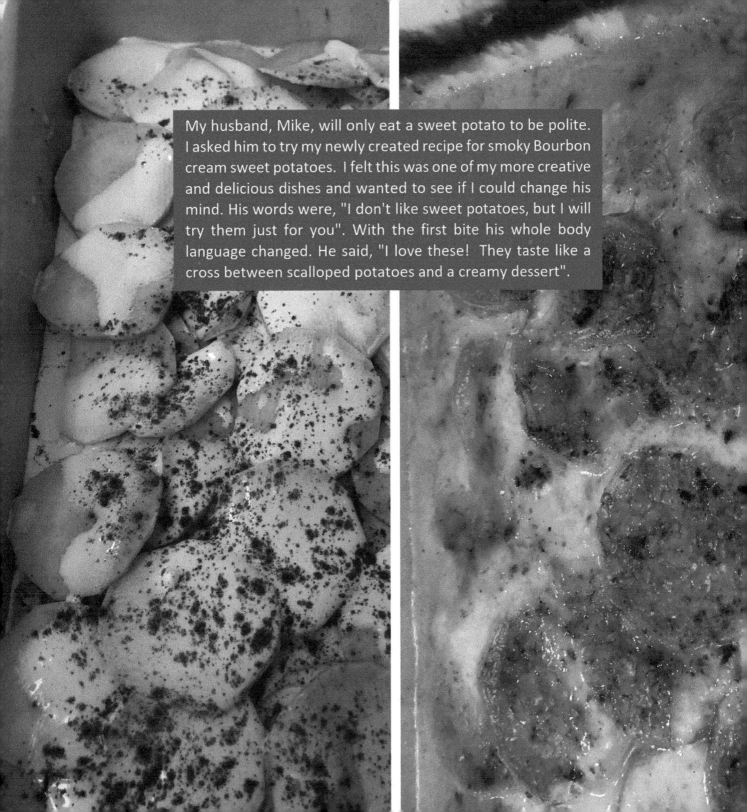

My husband, Mike, will only eat a sweet potato to be polite. I asked him to try my newly created recipe for smoky Bourbon cream sweet potatoes. I felt this was one of my more creative and delicious dishes and wanted to see if I could change his mind. His words were, "I don't like sweet potatoes, but I will try them just for you". With the first bite his whole body language changed. He said, "I love these! They taste like a cross between scalloped potatoes and a creamy dessert".

This is such a buttery pound cake that is so versatile! I first tasted Kentucky butter cake at Griffin Gate Resort in Lexington, Ky. It was generously covered with warm butter Bourbon sauce. I was so disappointed that my husband and I got the dessert to share – I really wanted a whole piece after I tasted the first bite. My grandmother had a recipe for butter pound cake, so I recreated the recipe after several tries and lots of Bourbon sauce to bring that same taste to my table. I serve thick slices topped with Bourbon butter sauce or caramel Bourbon sauce. It is my favorite base for strawberry short cake. The butter and strawberry juice mingle with vanilla ice cream - so smooth and yummy! Cake cubes in trifle with fresh berries or peaches layered with bourbon whipped cream is a way I have been able to pull together a quick and scrumptious dessert for drop-in guests. I keep several slices wrapped in the freezer for a quick dessert when I need one.

Butter Pound Cake with Bourbon Glaze

Butter Pound Cake

1 cup butter, room temperature (do not melt)

2 cups sugar

4 eggs

2 Tbsp Bourbon

3 cups all-purpose flour

1 tsp salt

1 tsp baking powder

½ tsp baking soda

1 cup buttermilk

Bourbon Butter Glaze

½ cup butter

¾ cup granulated sugar

**3 -7 Tbsp Bourbon
(3 Tbsp gives it a light Bourbon flavor,
 7 Tbsp gives it a strong Bourbon flavor)**

1 tsp vanilla

TIP: This cake is better made a day in advance or put it in your freezer for a couple of days. It makes the cake more moist.

You can eat this cake warm or cold. It warms nicely in the microwave and served with ice cream or whipped cream.

Preheat oven to 325 degrees. Grease or spray a Bundt or tube pan very liberally with baking spray or butter and flour.

For cake: Cream butter and sugar well. Add eggs and vanilla and mix well. Add the rest of the ingredients and mix well with a hand or stand mixer for 2-3 minutes.

Pour the batter into the prepared pan and bake for 70 minutes or until a knife comes out clean. Do not over bake. Watch closely starting at 60 minutes.

Do not remove the cake from the pan. You will be pouring the glaze into and on the cake while it is still in the pan.

For sauce: Melt the butter and sugar in a sauce pan until the sugar is melted. Do not let it boil. Remove from the heat and add vanilla and bourbon.

Make holes all over the bottom of the warm cake while it is still in the Bundt pan (avoiding the edges) using a knife and pour the glaze evenly on the cake.

Allow the cake to cool completely in the pan, then invert onto a cake plate or serving plate.

Dad's Favorite Manhattan

2 ounces of quality preferred Bourbon

1 ounce sweet vermouth

2 dashes of aromatic Bitters

1 maraschino cherry

¾ tsp maraschino cherry syrup

Place Bourbon and sweet vermouth in shaker containing ice.

Shake well for about 5 seconds and strain into a chilled cocktail glass.

Add two dashes of bitters with a maraschino cherry and cherry syrup, stir well.

Serve and enjoy.

Mike prepared a special treat for our guests at the taste testing!

My dad, Gerald Spencer, and my husband Mike have a long-time tradition of sharing a Manhattan each evening when we are at the house. When we arrive, dad looks at Mike with his thumbs up. Mike replies with his thumbs up and dad makes each a favorite Manhattan. You can find many versions of a Manhattan online and in books. While many of the ingredients are the same our family feels the cherry juice gives it a little different twist.

—Dayna

Fresh Apple Cake with Bourbon Nut Caramel Sauce

Fresh Apple Cake

2 cups sugar

½ cup unsweetened applesauce

½ cup canola oil

3 eggs

1 Tbsp Bourbon

2½ cups flour

1 tsp soda

1 tsp salt

2 tsp baking powder

3 Tbsp cinnamon

3½ cups finely chopped apples

1 cup course chopped walnuts

Bourbon Nut Caramel Sauce

14 oz can sweetened condensed milk

1 cup brown sugar

2 Tbsp butter

6 Tbsp Bourbon-soaked chopped pecans

TIP: Before starting the cake, soak 6 Tbsp chopped pecans in 6 Tbsp of Bourbon and set aside.

Preheat oven to 350 degrees. Spray a tube or Bundt pan with baking spray, or grease the pan and dust with flour.

For cake: Mix sugar, applesauce and oil until blended. Add eggs and bourbon and mix well.

Add the dry ingredients and mix well again

Stir in the apples and walnuts until evenly incorporated into the batter.

Bake at 350 degrees until a knife comes out clean from the center. Approximately 50 minutes depending on your oven.

For sauce: Combine milk and brown sugar in medium sauce pan and bring to a boil over medium-high heat stirring constantly.

Reduce heat and simmer for 8 minutes, stirring frequently. Remove from heat and add butter and bourbon-soaked pecans.

Let cool for 2-3 minutes. Drizzle on the cake while the topping is still hot.

Tiramisu is a favorite of mine – a cool and sophisticated dessert that is really easy to make, but looks very complicated. While I enjoy the rum version of this dessert, I am obsessed with the Bourbon and dark chocolate recipe I have created. It is a favorite go-to recipe in the summer that can be made ahead – actually better the second day! It lets me focus on my appetizers and main dishes without having to worry about the perfect ending. My guests go home feeling treated to a special dessert and usually there is at least a little left over for me!

Kentucky Tiramisu

Package of ladyfingers, roughly 12 oz

Bourbon Cream Chocolate Sauce

½ cup whipping cream

1½ Tbsp dark chocolate cocoa powder

**2 tsp instant espresso powder
(I use 2 packets of my favorite coffee shop's instant Italian dark roast coffee)**

1 small can sweetened condensed milk

1 cup Bourbon

1 tsp vanilla

Whipping Cream Layer

1 cup whipping cream

**8 oz package of cream cheese
(mascarpone is best if available)**

¼ cup granulated sugar

TIP: If the whipping cream mixture is too hard to spread, microwave it for about 10 seconds to soften it. If mixture is too firm it will tear the soaked ladyfingers.

For the Bourbon cream chocolate sauce: combine the cream, cocoa powder and espresso in a small pan. Turn on medium heat and stir or whisk constantly until the liquid is fully combined, about 2-3 minutes.

Cool for 5 minutes. Add the sweetened condensed milk, Bourbon and vanilla. Using a mixer, ensure the ingredients are blended together until creamy.

For the whipping cream layer: beat 1 cup whipping cream until it makes soft peaks. Stir in cream cheese (or mascarpone) and granulated sugar.

Line an 8x8 pan or dish with a single layer of ladyfingers split in the middle. Pour ¾ cup Bourbon cream chocolate sauce over ladyfingers ensuring each layer is soaked. Open the lady fingers to ensure the sauce fully soaks the ladyfingers.
Spread ½ of whipping cream layer mixture over top of soaked ladyfingers.

Add another layer of ladyfingers and repeat with bourbon cream chocolate sauce and whipping cream mixture.

Smooth the top layer of whipping cream and dust with dark chocolate powder. Chill for at least 4 hours before serving.

Manhattan Mushrooms

1 lb of mushrooms
(you can use whole mushrooms, caps or slices)

2 Tbsp butter

2 Tbsp sweet vermouth

2 Tbsp Bourbon

1 heaping tsp of minced garlic
(Tbsp of powdered garlic can be used)

TIP: These pair well with any steak.

Melt the butter in a medium skillet. Add mushrooms and minced garlic. Cook in butter until the mushrooms begin to soften

Add sweet vermouth and Bourbon and finish cooking until the desired mushroom consistency.

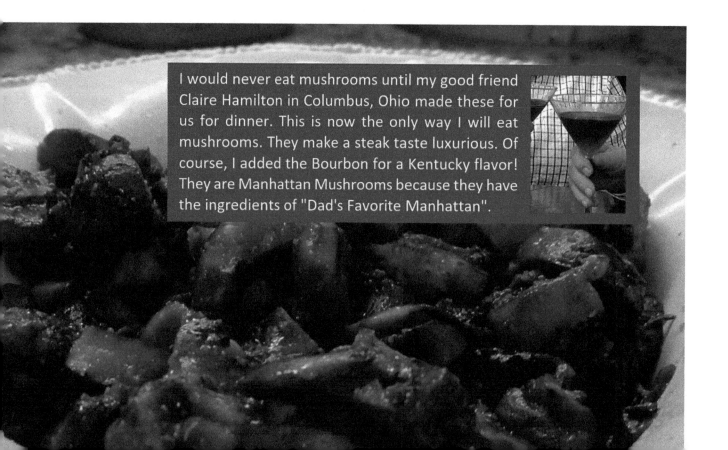

I would never eat mushrooms until my good friend Claire Hamilton in Columbus, Ohio made these for us for dinner. This is now the only way I will eat mushrooms. They make a steak taste luxurious. Of course, I added the Bourbon for a Kentucky flavor! They are Manhattan Mushrooms because they have the ingredients of "Dad's Favorite Manhattan".

Pork Tenderloin with Bourbon Cherry Glaze

Your favorite cut of pork tenderloin

½ cup sugar

½ tsp cinnamon

1 Tbsp flour

½ tsp salt

½ cup Bourbon

¼ cup light corn syrup

15 cherries - fresh, canned or frozen (not maraschino)

Preheat oven to 325 degrees. Place pork into large roasting dish (or this also works well in a crock pot). Tenderloins usually come two per package.

Rub a light coating of olive oil on the meat. Rub with salt, pepper and garlic. I typically use about 2 tsp of salt and about 3 tsp of garlic for two tenderloins.

Cook in the oven for 45 minutes to 1 hour. Check every 30 minutes - do not overcook.

Remove the meat and let it rest for about 15 minutes before slicing. While the meat is resting, prepare the cherry glaze.

Glaze: Place all ingredients into a large sauce pan and cook over medium heat until the sauce thickens.

Slice the meat and serve with the sauce.

While we love juicy pork tenderloin, we adore it with Bourbon cherry glaze! I have served it to friends who initially didn't want to put the cherry sauce on their pork who ended up finishing the sauce in the serving bowl with a spoon. I usually double the sauce recipe and put half in the refrigerator to have handy to pour over ice cream.

Bourbon Bacon Spaghetti Sauce

Spaghetti

6 oz spaghetti - your favorite thickness

2 lbs of 80/20 ground beef

Bourbon Bacon Sauce

4 oz of your favorite smoky BBQ sauce

1 can petite diced tomatoes

¼ cup Bourbon

¼ cup dark brown sugar

1 Tbsp of minced garlic

1 tsp salt

2 Tbsp pepper

3 Tbsp liquid smoke - hickory

1 Tbsp smoked paprika

2 tsp of Ancho ground chili pepper

**8 slices of bacon, cooked and crumbled
(use one package real bacon pieces if in a hurry)**

For sauce: Blend all sauce ingredients in a food processor or blender for about 15-20 seconds.

Place ground beef in skillet and cook over medium heat until just done, chopping into small pieces. Drain the beef and pat grease off using sturdy paper towels.

While you are cooking the hamburger prepare the spaghetti. Boil spaghetti (using your favorite shape or thickness). Be sure to drain well.

Place the meat and sauce in a large pan on top of the stove on low to medium heat for about 10 -15 minutes. Make sure you stir the sauce often or it will stick.

Place serving of spaghetti on plate and top with heaping serving of meat and sauce mixture. Garnish with your favorite cheese if desired.

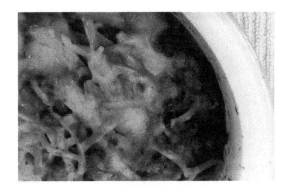

TIP: This recipe works well as either plated spaghetti or baked spaghetti. To make the baked version, I mix the sauce and spaghetti noodles thoroughly, then top with cheese. Since the sauce has a bit of a pop, I top the baked spaghetti with shredded pepper jack cheese the last few minutes of baking. I bake my spaghetti for about 30 minutes.

Holiday Carrots

8 large carrots cut into diagonal pieces. Some larger sections may need to be cut in two. (You can also use whole new carrots in the spring – like in the photo - for a pretty plate.)

¼ cup melted butter

¼ dark brown sugar

3 Tbsp Bourbon

Place carrots in a steamer bag in the microwave for about 2/3 of the recommended time.

Combine the butter and brown sugar in a pan and warm until sugar is melted.

Remove carrots from the steamer bag and put them in the pan with the other two ingredients.

Add the Bourbon.

Cook the carrots in the sauce until they can be pierced by a fork, but are not too soft to hold shape.

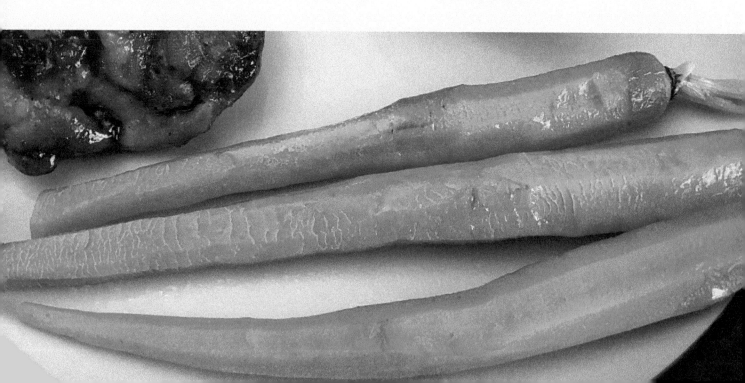

HOLIDAY
FAVORITES

The eggnog recipe you'll find in this book was shared by Martha Payne, a friend who adapted it from an Alton Brown recipe on the Food Network. For 7 years, it has been a part of the their December birthday and holiday dinner party. The original recipe uses uncooked eggs, however Martha has developed a cooked version. She and her husband Darren serve this as one of the dessert centerpieces of their party rather than just another drink option. It is always a big hit and her guests now request it each year. The Paynes serve it in a unique punch bowl with "12 Days of Christmas" cups made by Louisville Stoneware they bought at a silent auction fundraiser.

There are a number of recipes that people usually make during the holidays. I invite you to try some of those favorites at other times of the year. And, one of your new favorites you find in this book just might end up being a new holiday tradition!

The cake shown here is a twist on the traditional Yule Log cake. I always thought something was missing when I ate a Yule Log -- not enough flavor. Then I decided to add bourbon-soaked nuts to the cream cheese center.

This is a Yule Log that brought much more cheer to our family table than the traditional version! My grandmother had a white chocolate cake recipe made with buttermilk that was perfect to roll for the cake portion of the Yule Log.

I adapted my grandmother's recipe and used dark chocolate to make a springy cake that is perfect with the bourbon cream cheese icing filling and chocolate bourbon icing. Enjoy!

Christmas Bourbon Yule Log

Cake

6 large eggs, separated

¼ tsp cream of tartar

⅛ tsp salt

¾ cup white sugar

⅓ cup all-purpose flour

½ cup unsweetened dark cocoa powder

½ tsp baking powder

1 tsp vanilla

Powdered sugar

Filling

8 oz cream cheese, room temperature

3 Tbsp Bourbon-soaked pecans

16 oz confectioners sugar

Chocolate Ganache

½ cup whipping cream

1 cup dark chocolate chips

1 Tbsp light corn syrup

1 tsp Bourbon

Heat oven to 375 degrees. Line the bottom of a 15x10x1 pan with non-stick foil or parchment paper. Spray pan bottom and sides with baking spray, line the bottom of the pan with wax paper and coat paper with spray.

For cake: In a large bowl, combine egg whites, cream of tarter and salt until peaks form. Add ¼ cup of sugar gradually.

In another bowl combine yolks with vanilla and ½ cup sugar and beat until thick.

Combine cocoa, flour and baking powder in a small bowl. Combine well before adding to other ingredients.

Fold yolks into the egg whites, then add the dry ingredients slowly until all are thoroughly combined.

Spread the batter evenly on the prepared pan. Bake for 10-12 minutes until it lightly springs back to the touch. This cake cooks very fast so watch it carefully.

Loosen the edges of the cake. Lightly sprinkle the top of the cake with confectioners sugar. Turn the cake over onto a clean dish towel. While still hot, roll the cake up very carefully. Set aside to cool completely.

For filling: Using a mixer, beat the 3 ingredients until the consistency of icing.

Once cake is cooled, unroll the cake and spread the filling evenly over the inside of the cake. Roll the cake back up, setting the seam on the bottom.

For ganache: Heat whipping cream in the microwave for one minute. Take out of the microwave and add light corn syrup and chocolate chips. Use a whisk until smooth. Add Bourbon and whisk again. You may have to put the mixture in the refrigerator for a few minutes to get the consistence you need for spreading the frosting.

Use a fork to make "bark swirls" in the ganache to resemble a log.

Eggnog

Serves 6 to 7 cups

4 egg yolks

⅓ cup sugar, plus 1 tablespoon sugar

2 cups whole milk (don't skimp by using low-fat or 2% - we use high quality organic milk)

1 cup heavy cream

3 ounces any high-quality Bourbon

1 tsp freshly grated nutmeg (use whole nutmeg; freshly grated adds nice texture and better flavor!)

4 egg whites (refrigerate for later use)

Separate eggs and refrigerate the whites for later. Use a mixer and beat the egg yolks until they lighten in color. Gradually add 1/3 cup sugar and continue to beat until completely dissolved. Set aside.

In saucepan, combine milk, heavy cream and nutmeg and bring just to a boil, stirring occasionally. Remove from heat immediately at first sign of a boil. Gradually add the hot mixture to the egg and sugar mixture, stirring well.

Return everything to saucepan and cook until the mixture reaches 160 degrees using a candy thermometer. Stir occasionally to make sure it does not boil.

Remove from heat and stir in the Bourbon and pour into a large mixing bowl and set in the refrigerator to chill for several hours (or even overnight).

Close to serving time beat the egg whites to soft peaks. With the mixer running, gradually add the remaining 1 tablespoon of sugar and beat until stiff peaks form. Fold the egg whites into the cooked chilled mixture. Refrigerate until ready to serve.

I adore Bourbon Creams as Grandmother Spencer would call them – she would *never* call them Bourbon Balls. I have eaten many versions, but then lucked into finding someone who made them with enough Bourbon to make me want to eat several. Dr. Rex Chaney, a Morehead State professor, made Bourbon Balls with filling that oozed in your mouth when you bit into them and exploded with flavor, warming your insides on the way down. While I could pry out some details of his process, he didn't use a formal recipe. Thus began a twenty-year quest of trying new combinations, new chocolates, different Bourbons and roasting pecans. What you see here is the final result – *and you may never again eat any other Bourbon Ball!*

Bourbon Balls

This is the recipe that started it all! My passion for trying new recipes and my love of sharing them with family and friends both began with perfecting these delicious treats.
—Dayna

Makes about 30 amazing Bourbon Balls

1 cup of Bourbon-soaked chopped pecan mixture (see tip)

½ cup softened, not melted, butter

16 oz confectioners sugar

**2 pkgs dark chocolate melting wafers for candy making and dipping
(I prefer to use high-quality name brand melting wafers as they offer the perfect consistency to add a light layer of dark chocolate – remember, I have done a lot of testing!)**

**30 whole pecans
(I roast mine first which gives them a better favor)**

Toothpicks

TIP: Prepare Bourbon-soaked chopped pecan mixture at least 2 days before making Bourbon Balls. Add 1½ cups Bourbon to cover 2 cups finely chopped pecans. Seal in jar or container with lid. Store leftover mixture to use up to a month later – like when you make my Bourbon Ball Cake to wow your friends!

TIP: Each Bourbon Ball has on average ½ shot of Bourbon, so be sure NOT to eat and drive!

Mix butter, Bourbon-soaked nuts and sugar together until smooth. Do not add more sugar – the mixture will be very thin. Place in the refrigerator (sealed) for at least 4 hours.

Line cookie sheet with parchment or wax paper. Use a small melon ball dipper to make uniform balls. Scoop, then flatten on the bottom. Place on prepared cookie sheet. Place in freezer for 1 hour.

Place 10 oz of chocolate in small container deep enough to dip whole candy ball to cover top. Follow the instructions on chocolate on how to melt – go slow to make sure it does not burn and clump.

Take the frozen candy out of freezer. Insert toothpick in top and dip into chocolate, covering entire candy. Hold dipped candy sideways over container to allow excess chocolate to drip off. Set the candy back on cookie sheet. Use another toothpick to gently remove the toothpick in the candy and place a whole pecan on the top.

Place cookie sheet in refrigerator to set the chocolate. These should be stored in a cool place. Then set out and serve at room temperature for best flavor.

Tipsy Pecan Cake

This is my Great-Grandmother Spencer's recipe. It can be served with one of my Bourbon sauces, or try wrapping it in Bourbon-soaked cheesecloth and serve it as a fruitcake.
   —Dayna

2 cups granulated sugar

1 ½ sticks butter (¾ cup), softened

6 eggs

4 cups of flour or 5 cups of cake flour

2 Tbsp nutmeg

1 heaping Tbsp of baking powder

½ cup sorghum or dark corn syrup (your preference)

1 lb pecans, chopped in large pieces

1 cup Bourbon - of course!

For the pecan Bourbon "no fruit" fruitcake:

Wrap the cake in cheesecloth lightly soaked in Bourbon and then cover with plastic wrap.

Place in the refrigerator for 2 days.

Remove from refrigerator and repeat the process 2 more times.

Store in the refrigerator for at least a week before serving. It will be worth the wait!

Preheat oven to 275 degrees.

Place a metal rectangle cake pan ¾ full of water on the bottom rack.

Prepare a Bundt pan with baking spray or butter and flour (always my choice).

Cream the sugar and softened butter together using a mixer.

Add in the eggs one at a time and mix thoroughly.

Add dry ingredients and mix well.

Add sorghum or dark corn syrup and the Bourbon and mix on high for 1 minute.

Add pecans and mix thoroughly, distributing the pecans evenly.

Pour the batter in the Bundt pan. It will be extremely full and will bake above the pan.

It takes about an hour in a convection oven.

During the last 15 minutes check the cake periodically with a knife. When it comes out clean, the cake is done.

SAUCES, GLAZES & CREAMS

Be adventuresome and experiment using these different sauces, glazes and creams to enhance the flavor of the foods you love. You will find them in many of the recipes throughout the book. It has taken a number of tries to get just the right combinations so they are not too sharp or lacking in distinctive Bourbon flavor. I hope you enjoy them and I am sure you will think of many more uses for these flavorful additions to your favorite dishes.

—Dayna

Bourbon Nut Caramel Sauce

14 oz can sweetened condensed milk

1 cup brown sugar

2 Tbsp butter

6 Tbsp Bourbon-soaked chopped pecans (cover 6 Tbsp of pecans with 6 Tbsp of Bourbon and allow them to soak)

Combine milk and brown sugar in medium sauce pan and bring to a boil over medium high heat stirring constantly. Reduce heat and simmer for 8 minutes, stirring frequently. Remove from heat and add butter and Bourbon-soaked pecans. Let cool for 2-3 minutes. Drizzle on cake while the topping is hot.

Whipped Bourbon Cream

1 cup heavy cream, chilled

1½ Tbsp Bourbon

1 tsp sugar

Whip the heavy cream with mixer until stiff peaks appear. Stir in sugar and Bourbon and serve immediately.

Chocolate Bourbon Sauce

1 cup granulated sugar

½ stick butter (¼ cup)

1 small can evaporated milk

1 egg

¼ cup Bourbon

¼ cup dark chocolate syrup

Combine first four ingredients and cook in a double boiler until slightly thick. Remove from heat and let it cool.

Add in chocolate and Bourbon. Use a mixer until smooth and store in a jar with lid.

Keeps for weeks in a glass jar with lid in the refrigerator. You can use over ice cream or bread pudding.

Chocolate Ganache

½ cup whipping cream

1 cup dark chocolate chips

1 Tbsp light corn syrup

1 tsp Bourbon

Heat whipping cream in microwave for 1 minute. Take out of microwave and add light corn syrup and chocolate chips. Use a whisk until smooth. Add Bourbon and whisk again. You may have to put mixture in the refrigerator for a few minutes to get the consistency you need to spread the frosting. Store any leftovers in refrigerator.

Cream Cheese Icing

8 oz cream cheese, softened

½ cup butter, softened

2 Tbsp Bourbon

4 cups confectioners sugar

Put first three ingredients into large mixing bowl. Add one cup of sugar at a time and beat until well blended and the consistency of icing. Make sure your cake or dessert is cool or icing will run.

TIP: For Cherry Cream Cheese Icing, I omit 1 Tbsp of Bourbon and add ½ cup of Bourbon-soaked maraschino cherries.

Creamy Bourbon Sauce

TIP: This works well over bread pudding, cake or fruit.

4 oz cream cheese

2 Tbsp butter, melted

1 cup confectioners sugar

¼ cup of Bourbon

Using a mixer, cream all four ingredients together and drizzle over bread pudding. If it is a bit stiff, try putting it in the microwave for 10 seconds at a time.

Cherry Bourbon Glaze

TIP: This can be used on ice cream, as a sauce for cake, and for pork tenderloin.

½ cup sugar

½ tsp cinnamon

1 Tbsp flour

½ tsp salt

½ cup Bourbon

¼ cup light corn syrup

15 cherries - fresh, canned or frozen (no maraschino cherries)

Place all ingredients into a large sauce pan and cook over medium heat until the sauce thickens. (For a stronger Bourbon flavor, add 1 Tbsp of Bourbon after you remove it from the heat.)

Bourbon Pecan Glaze

1 cup light corn syrup

¼ cup sugar

½ stick butter (¼ cup)

¾ cup Bourbon-soaked chopped pecans (¾ cup nuts and ½ cup Bourbon)

Combine first three ingredients and stir over medium heat until sugar is dissolved. Cook for 1 minute after rolling boil begins. Remove from heat and add in ¾ cup of Bourbon-soaked chopped pecans.

Stores well in the refrigerator. Reheat to drizzle over your favorite desserts.

Bourbon Brown Sugar Butter

1 stick butter, softened at room temperature

3 Tbsp dark brown sugar

2 Tbsp Bourbon

Combine the ingredients. It is wonderful on pancakes, biscuits and yeast rolls!

Bourbon Butter

(for steak, pork tenderloin or roasts)

1 stick butter, softened

1 Tbsp garlic

2 Tbsp Bourbon

Season meat with salt and pepper. Let the meat sit for about 15 minutes to absorb the seasoning.

Combine ingredients. Cover meat with a layer of the Bourbon butter. You can grill or oven roast the meat. The final dish will be a juicier and much more tender cut.

Since the early nineteenth century this butter dish has graced the Spencer table for meals. It was inherited from my great-grandparents, William Knox and Elizabeth Spencer. It is an English antique silver covered butter dish with a compartment below the butter for crushed ice to keep butter solid, because houses at that time did not have air conditioning. My mom and dad use it for most of our family get-togethers. It is not just saved for special dinners, rather our family believes special pieces are to be used often. And special dishes with Bourbon can become favorites – *and not just when company is coming!*

Index

Conversion Charts

Liquid Equivalents		
1/4 tsp	=	1 ml
1/2 tsp	=	2 ml
1 tsp	=	5 ml
1 Tbls	=	15 ml
2 Tbls	=	30 ml
1/4 cup	=	60 ml
1/3 cup	=	80 ml
1/2 cup	=	120 ml
2/3 cup	=	160 ml
3/4 cup	=	180 ml
1 cup	=	240 ml

Standard Cup Equivalents		Flour	Sugar	Butter	Milk
1/8 cup	=	19 g	24 g	25 g	30 ml
1/4 cup	=	38 g	48 g	50 g	60 ml
1/3 cup	=	50 g	63 g	67 g	80 ml
1/2 cup	=	75 g	95 g	100 g	120 ml
2/3 cup	=	100 g	125 g	133 g	160 ml
3/4 cup	=	113 g	143 g	150 g	180 ml
1 cup	=	150 g	190 g	200 g	240 ml

Temperatures		
275 ° F	=	135 ° C
300 ° F	=	150 ° C
325 ° F	=	160 ° C
350 ° F	=	180 ° C
375 ° F	=	190 ° C

Dayna Seelig is a retired professor of 27 years from Morehead State University. She was raised to appreciate traditional southern cuisine that included canning, preserving and cooking with her grandmothers. She was raised in Lexington and on a thoroughbred horse farm in Flemingsburg, Kentucky.

Cooking and baking provide a relaxing outlet for her creative energies and she loves to watch her friends and family enjoy each other around a table of food.

She lives in Mt. Sterling, Kentucky with her husband, Mike. Both sons, Rian Brown and Justin Brown, are wonderful cooks and have their own specialty items. And the tradition is being passed along to the next generation. The first question her two grandchildren, Hadlee and Quinn Brown, ask as soon as they come to her house is "what do we get to bake today?".

Dayna can be followed at www.kentuckyspiritedchef.com or on Facebook as The Kentucky Spirited Chef.

Jeffrey Liles is owner of Mound Marketing & Communications LLC. Previously, he worked for the Lexington Herald-Leader, where he learned about publishing and also worked with great writers and columnists.

Dayna first met Jeffrey at Morehead State University, where he served as assistant vice president for marketing, responsible for the University's publications.

In his hometown, he has published the Mt. Sterling-Montgomery County Chamber of Commerce magazine. He currently co-hosts a TV show, Mound Magazine TV, that airs monthly on Lexington's WTVQ ABC-Channel 36.

This is the first cookbook Jeffrey has helped publish. While the layout and design work was always filled with appealing photos and descriptions, the taste testings and food sample deliveries that Dayna provided on a regular basis made it an especially appetizing project.

CPSIA information can be obtained
at www.ICGtesting.com
Printed in the USA
LVHW070509081021
699748LV00001B/1